MW00935212

THE MYSTERIOUS DISAPPEARANCE

Why the Pre-Tribulation Rapture is a Fundamental Doctrine of Biblical Prophecy

Written by Dr. Daniel R. Carfrey

PRESS

The Mysterious Disappearance
Why the Pre-Tribulation Rapture is a Fundamental
Doctrine of Biblical Prophecy
by Dr. Daniel R. Carfrey

Printed in the United States of America

ISBN 978-1-60647-683-3

www.xulonpress.com

ACKNOWLEDGEMENTS

B eing my first published book, I would like to acknowledge the following as having had a positive impact in my life pertaining to my spiritual life and development, going all the way back to my early childhood in Arizona: My parents, Rev. Charles and Mary Carfrey; Dr. Dick Mercado, Rev. Clayton Hull, Dr. Carl Hodges, Bob Jones University, Rev. Sam Staggs, Dr. Don Wilson, Rev. James Bender, Dallas Theological Seminary, and Baptist Bible Seminary.

I would like to thank the many fundamental local churches and friends who have supported our ministry down through the years, to include Pastor Pat Haynes and the members of Hilltop Baptist Church in which my wife and I currently serve the Lord. I would like to thank as well the many former folks who have sat under my ministry, as well as the many former students in the classroom, who have strongly encouraged me to put into print that which I have been teaching and preaching.

I am deeply grateful for the privilege of having served on the faculty here at Appalachian Bible College these past seventeen years. A special thanks to Dr. Daniel Anderson, President; Dr. Charles Bethel, Academic Dean; and Mr. Ed Chesley, our Librarian who assisted me in editing this material. Also this book would not have been made available at this time without the help of Frank and Jane Turpin, good friends and supporters for many years..

Finally, I am grateful to the Lord for His gift to me of my wife Shirley, and my daughter MarySusan.

TABLE OF CONTENTS

PREFACE

The term "Pre-Tribulation Rapture" refers to a theological position that claims the Church age believers will be caught up suddenly into heaven to be with the Lord in the air, whether their bodies are asleep in Christ at the time, or whether they be living at the moment the event occurs. God's purpose for the Rapture is to deliver the Church age saints from the Tribulation, or the time of God's wrath upon the nations of the world which is to follow the Rapture. This will be the sudden *mysterious disappearance* of millions of Christians on every continent, <u>all at once</u>!

The purpose for this book is two-fold. **First**, it is to give reasons why it is important to believe in the doctrine of the Pre-Tribulation Rapture of the Church. It has been the joy of this writer to sit under the teachings of some of the premier teachers of biblical prophecy. I have sat under the teachings of Dr. Charles Ryrie, Dr. Dwight Pentecost, and the late Dr. John Walvoord—all well-known prophetic scholars. I have also been exposed to the teachings of Dr. Renald Showers in this area of doctrine as well. Every one of these Bible believing scholars and authors hold to the Pre-Tribulation theological position, and everyone of them agree that a time of Tribulation follows the Rapture—to include the seven years yet to be fulfilled upon the nation of Israel as spoken of by the prophet Daniel.

This writer believes the theological position they advocate to be sound biblically. In fact, this writer believes the Scriptures themselves point to the Pre-Tribulation Rapture as being a fundamental to hold on to, and to not distort or deny. It is the purpose of this book to demonstrate this to be a fact.

The **second purpose** for this book is *to address some disagreements between Pre-Tribulation Rapture scholars*, though they be minor compared to those who deny the Pre-Tribulation position. It is to be acknowledged that not all agree upon the exact sequence of events that occurs from the time of the Rapture to the return of Christ back to this earth. This lack of agreement is due to an assumption by many that the total time of the Tribulation lasts only those seven years mentioned by the prophet Daniel. It is an alternative to that viewpoint that this writer would like to present for consideration, because it offers a resolution to those disagreements between fundamental Pre-Tribulation scholars.

The chapters which follow are presented in a logical order, building a case step-by-step to fulfill these two purposes. It would be better therefore to not skip chapters, but to read them in the order they are presented. Whether one agrees or not with the alternative view this writer presents regarding the sequence of events during the Tribulation, the fact that the Rapture of the Church occurs before any portion of the Tribulation begins is clear from Scripture. One should therefore be on guard against any effort to undermine this "blessed hope" of the believer today.

CHAPTER ONE

IT IS A DIVINE MYSTERY PERTAINING TO THE CHURCH

Introduction

The Bible is not one book, but a collection of sixty-six books, all written by holy men who were inspired by the one true God. Not all of God's truth was revealed at one time in human history. It is therefore important to research all of God's Word as to what is stated pertaining to a certain doctrine or topic.

In order to understand the Rapture of the Church, it is helpful to know what God has revealed about the resurrection of the dead in general. To do this, we will first look at what God told the prophet Daniel pertaining to the two kinds of resurrection; what Jesus had to say about the order of the two resurrections when He was on the earth; the information the apostle Paul added after Christ's ascension into heaven, pertaining to stages in the first resurrection; and finally the time interval between the two resurrections as revealed to the apostle John in the last book of the New Testament.

The Two Kinds of Resurrection

The prophet Daniel wrote about two different kinds of resurrection in the latter days. He said that many of those whose bodies lie in the dust of death would arise, but not all to the same destiny. Some would rise to eternal salvation, and some to eternal condemnation.

And many of them that sleep in the dust of the earth shall awake, some to everlasting life, and some to shame and everlasting contempt. Daniel 12:2.

The prophet did not state any further details, such as whether or not the resurrection unto salvation and the resurrection unto condemnation would occur at once. It would be the Lord Jesus Himself, when He was on the earth, who would give further details as to the order of the two kinds of resurrection.

The Order of the Two Resurrections

Jesus, in defending His ministry to those who opposed Him, claimed that the Father had committed all judgment into His hands, in order that man might honor Him equally with the Father Who sent Him.

For as the Father raiseth up the dead, and quickeneth them; even so the Son quickeneth whom he will. For the Father judgeth no man, but hath committed all judgment unto the Son: That all men should honour the Son, even as they honour the Father. He that honoureth not the Son honoureth not the Father which hath sent him. John 5:21-23.

Jesus then declared that those who believed in Him before they died, and believed in the Father Who sent Him, would hear His voice in the future when He first calls forth the dead to eternal life and salvation.

Verily, verily, I say unto you, He that heareth my word, and believeth on him that sent me, hath everlasting life, and shall not come into condemnation, but is passed from death unto life. Verily, verily, I say unto you, The hour is coming, and now is, when the dead shall hear the voice of the Son of God: and they that hear shall live. For as the Father hath life in himself; so hath he given to the Son to have life in himself; John 5:24-26.

Notice some key phrases in these verses. "Verily, verily" means "Truly, truly." In other words, what Jesus has to say about the future resurrection unto life eternal can be counted on. The phrase, "I say unto you," emphasizes the fact that it is Jesus, as God's judge, who will determine those that will be raised unto life eternal in the future, and those who will not. Notice that Jesus does not say that all will hear His voice when He calls forth the dead unto everlasting life. He says "they that hear shall live." In other words, the key to hearing the Lord's voice when He calls forth the dead unto everlasting life and salvation, is one's willingness to hear His word and believe in Him before death!

But one might ask, "What about the rest of the dead who are not raised unto everlasting life and salvation?" Jesus says they too will hear the voice of the Son of God calling them forth from the graves, but instead of being given everlasting life based upon their faith in Him, they will be condemned on the basis of their own works.

And hath given him authority to execute judgment also, because he is the Son of man. Marvel not at this: for the hour is coming, in the which all that are in the graves shall hear his voice, And shall come forth; they that have done good, unto the resurrection of life; and they that have done evil, unto the resurrection of damnation. John 5:27-29.

Note the contrast between the words "they that hear" in verse twenty-five, and the words "all that are in the graves shall hear" in verse twenty-eight. The "all" refers to the rest of the dead who did not hear the first time Jesus called forth the dead to life. This is the second time He calls forth the dead, only this time it will not be to everlasting life, but everlasting condemnation. The basis for their judgment will be their own works on which they must stand, *having first rejected the person and work of Jesus Christ on their behalf to save them.* God will be fair. If a person <u>always</u> did that which is good, he will earn eternal life. But if he <u>ever</u> did that which is evil, he will be raised unto damnation. The apostle Paul emphasized this fact to the Romans as well. (Compare Romans 2:5-11).

So Jesus emphasized again what had been revealed many years before to the prophet Daniel, and that is there are two general kinds of resurrection. One kind is unto eternal life, and the other kind is unto eternal condemnation. But man learned further from the lips of Christ that the two resurrections do not occur at the same time. Rather, the resurrection unto life will be first for those who have placed their faith in Jesus alone for salvation, and not in their own works. This will be followed later by the resurrection unto condemnation for those who will be judged for their works.

Hence the order of the two kinds of resurrection. The first general resurrection will be unto eternal salva-

tion. And the second resurrection will be unto eternal damnation.

The Stages of the First Resurrection

After Christ ascended into heaven, it was revealed to the apostle Paul that the first resurrection unto everlasting life would not be all at once. It would occur in stages. The first stage would be the resurrection of Christ Himself as the first fruits; the second stage would involve those who belonged to Christ at His coming; and the third stage would take place at the time of the end, when Jesus Christ returns to reign upon this earth prior to its eventual destruction.

For as in Adam all die, even so in Christ shall all be made alive. But every man in his own order: Christ the firstfruits; afterward they that are Christ's at his coming. Then cometh the end, when he shall have delivered up the kingdom to God, even the Father; when he shall have put down all rule and all authority and power. For he must reign till he hath put all enemies under his feet. The last enemy that shall be destroyed is death. 1 Corinthians 15:22-26.

Notice that there are two comings of Christ mentioned by the apostle. The first is for those who belong to Him as part of the Church, when He calls for them to join Him in the air. Paul will amplify this in his epistle to the Thessalonians (see below). The second is when He returns back to this present earth to conquer all of God's enemies, and bring it under subjection to God. It is at this same time that Daniel was told the resurrection unto life would occur for Old Testament saints (Daniel 12:1-2). From that time forth, no believers left upon the earth will die, proving that Christ has conquered death as the last enemy of mankind (1 Corinthians 15:25-26).

The Mystery Associated with the Rapture of the Church

In discussing the three stages of the first resurrection unto life, Paul emphasizes that the body of the saints who are raised to join Christ in the air will be changed from that which is earthly, to that which is heavenly; from that which is natural or soulish (depending upon blood to sustain life) to that which is spiritual; from that which is corruptible to that which is incorruptible; from that which is patterned after Adam, whose body was formed from the "dust of the ground" (The name Adam as being derived from the Hebrew word *Adamah,* meaning the ground), to that which is patterned after the Lord from heaven. This is because flesh and blood, in its present corrupted state, is not designed to live in heaven. It must be changed. 1 Corinthians 15:42-50.

It is in light of this necessary change that the apostle reveals a mystery pertaining to the resurrection of the Church age saints. Those who are living and belong to Christ will be instantly changed without dying, so that they can join deceased loved ones in Christ who are raised at that time, to meet the Lord in the air.

Behold, I shew you a mystery; We shall not all sleep, but we shall all be changed. In a moment, in the twinkling of an eye, at the last trump: for the trumpet shall sound, and the dead shall be raised incorruptible, and we shall be changed. For this corruptible must put on incorruption, and this mortal must put on immortality. 1 Corinthians 15:51-53.

Paul further describes this event to the Thessalonian believers.

For this we say unto you by the word of the Lord, that we which are alive and remain unto the coming of the Lord shall not prevent (or precede) them which are asleep. For the Lord himself shall descend from heaven with a shout, with the voice of the archangel, and with the trump of God: and the dead in Christ shall rise first: Then we which are alive and remain shall be caught up together with them in the clouds, to meet the Lord in the air: and so shall we ever be with the Lord. 1 Thessalonians 4:15-17.

Note two things about the words "we which are alive and remain shall be caught up together with them in the clouds." First, the word "rapture" is taken from the Latin translation for the words "caught up." It means those raptured will be caught up into heaven in a moment, in the twinkling of an eye, without dying, to meet the Lord in the air. Second, Paul was anticipating that the Rapture could occur at any time, for he included himself as perhaps being one of those still alive on earth when the dead in Christ arose first ("*we* which are alive and remain").

The doctrine of the Rapture of the Church is called a "mystery" by the apostle Paul. This is because the Rapture applies to the Church-age saints, and was therefore not revealed to Israel in Old Testament times. It is also a mystery, in that this is the only time in which saints who are alive are instantly changed and caught up to meet the Lord in the air, without first dying.

The Time Interval Between the Two Resurrections

It is in the last book of the Bible that God revealed to the apostle John the time period between the first and second resurrection. John writes that those who are martyred for their faith in Christ during the Tribulation will be raised at the end when Christ returns to reign upon this earth. They will be rewarded for their suffering by reigning with Christ for one thousand years. This will be the final stage of the first resurrection unto life (Revelation 20:4).

John pronounces a blessing upon all those raised in the first resurrection unto life eternal, saying that they will not experience the second death unto condemnation.

Blessed and holy is he that hath part in the first resur-rection: on such the second death hath no power... Revelation 20:6.

But as for the rest of the dead, John says they will remain in the grave until Christ's reign for one thousand years is completed (Revelation 20:5). It is only after the first one thousand years of Christ's reign that Satan will be loosed (Revelation 20:7-9) and then cast into hell (Revelation 20:10), that the rest of the dead will be raised to be condemned for their works.

And I saw a great white throne, and him that sat on it, from whose face the earth and the heaven fled away; and there was found no place for them. And I saw the dead, small and great, stand before God; and the books were opened: and another book was opened, which is the book of life: and the dead were judged out of those things which were written in the books, according to their works... And death and hell were cast into the lake of fire. This is the second death. And whosoever was not found written in the book of life was cast into the lake of fire. Revelation 20:11-12, 14-15.

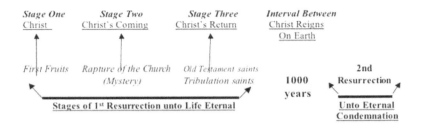

<u>Illustrative Chart of Two General Resurrections</u>

<u>Summary</u>

So one of the reasons the Pre-Tribulational Rapture is a fundamental doctrine to be guarded and cherished by the church today, is because it is a <u>divine mystery</u> pertaining to the unique dispensation in which believers now live, called the "Church Age." There are reasons God will cause a *mysterious disappearance* to occur <u>all at once</u>, of millions of true believers in Jesus Christ from around the world. A major reason for this sudden disappearance will be discussed in Chapter Two.

IT SIGNALS THE BEGINNING OF THE TRIBULATION

Introduction

Pressure and suffering are part of one's experience in this world of sin. Jesus told His disciples that they would suffer tribulation in this world, but to be of good cheer in that He has overcome the world (John 16:33). Yet there is coming a day in which the whole world will go through a period of uncommon suffering. It will be a time of God's outpoured wrath upon all the nations of the world for their sin. This time period is commonly termed by theologians as "The Tribulation."

When speaking of the future Tribulation prior to Christ's return, one must distinguish between God's judgment upon the <u>whole world</u> of nations for their sins, and seven years <u>Israel</u> has yet to pay for her <u>past</u> <u>sins</u> as revealed to the prophet Daniel. Once we have observed the difference, we will then examine Christ's words in His Olivet Discourse pertaining to the time period for the Tribulation as a whole, and how the mystery of the Rapture is related to it.

The Coming Tribulation upon the World of Nations

The prophets of old were warned of a time period called "day of the Lord," in which God would judge His people for their sins by delivering them into captivity to Gentile nations. The prophet Joel was probably the first to mention it.

Alas for the day! For the day of the Lord is at hand, and as a destruction from the Almighty shall it come. Joel 1:15.

In like manner specific Gentile nations were warned of a day of God's judgment to come upon them. These prophecies were fulfilled against the enemies of God and of Israel such as Babylon, Assyria, Moab, Edom.

But there is a special "day of the Lord" yet to be fulfilled of which the prophets spoke. They foretold of a day in which the Lord would pour out His undiluted wrath upon the whole world of nations for their idolatry and for their sin.

Enter into the rock, and hide thee in the dust, for fear of the Lord, and for the glory of his majesty. The lofty looks of man shall be humbled, and the haughtiness of men shall be bowed down, and the Lord alone shall be exalted in that day. For the day of the Lord of hosts shall be upon every one that is proud and lofty, and upon every one that is lifted up; and he shall be brought low...And they shall go into the holes of the rocks, and into the caves of the earth, for fear of the Lord, and for the glory of his majesty, when he ariseth to shake terribly the earth. In that day a man shall cast his idols of silver, and his idols of gold, which they made each one for himself to worship, to the moles and to the bats; To go into the clefts of the rocks, and into the tops of the ragged rocks, for fear of the Lord, and for the glory of his majesty, when he ariseth to shake terribly the earth. Isaiah 2:10-12, 17-21.

Howl ye; for the day of the Lord is at hand; it shall come as a destruction from the Almighty. Therefore shall all hands be faint, and every man's heart shall melt: And they shall be afraid: pangs and sorrows shall take hold of them; they shall be in pain as a woman that travaileth: they shall be amazed one at another; their faces shall be as flames. Behold, the day of the Lord cometh, cruel both with wrath and fierce anger, to lay the land desolate: and he shall destroy the sinners thereof out of it. For the stars of heaven and the constellations thereof shall not give their light: the sun shall be darkened in his going forth, and the moon shall not cause her light to shine. And I will punish the world for their evil, and the wicked for their iniquity; and I will cause the arrogancy of the proud to cease, and will lay low the haughtiness of the terrible. I will make a man more precious than fine gold; even a man than the golden wedge of Ophir. Therefore I will shake the heavens, and the earth shall remove out of her place, in the wrath of the Lord of hosts, and in the day of his fierce anger. Isaiah 12:6-13.

It should be obvious that this "day of the Lord" has not yet been fulfilled. More details of this future time period are given in the book of Revelation, which is the subject of the next chapter. The whole Gentile world will suffer for their sins. God's wrath is building. The cup of His indignation is filling up. And the nation of Israel will not escape for her own national sins at that time. But this is <u>not to be confused</u>

with a special time of suffering Israel has yet to pay for her
past sins.

The Seven Year Tribulation upon the Nation of Israel

The prophet Jeremiah foretold the day when the nation
Israel would go into captivity to the nation Babylon for
seventy years.

*And this whole land shall be a desolation, and an
astonishment; and these nations shall serve the king
of Babylon seventy years. Jeremiah 25:11.*

When the seventy years were about to be accomplished,
the prophet Daniel besought the Lord to have mercy and
restore the glory of Israel. He was told instead that the nation
would suffer seven times more, or seventy years times seven,
for the remaining sins of the nation against the Law, after
which Israel would be restored to its glory under the reign of
the coming Messiah.

*Seventy weeks are determined upon thy people and
upon the holy city, to finish the transgression, and to
make an end of sins, and to make reconciliation for
iniquity, and to bring in everlasting righteousness,
and to seal up the vision and prophecy, and to anoint
the most Holy. Daniel 9:24.*

It should be noted that the "seventy weeks," as translated
in the King James Version, is literally "seventy sevens" in
the Hebrew text, and refers to the seventy years mentioned
by Daniel in verse two as being intensified seven times
more. This is consistent with God's warnings to Israel in
establishing His covenant with the nation, in that He foretold

punishing them seven times more for not repenting when He sought to correct them through national discipline.

And if ye will not yet for all this hearken unto me, then I will punish you seven times more for your sins. Leviticus 26:18 (The same is repeated in 26:21, 24, and 28).

The angel Gabriel went on to inform Daniel that the total time—from the command permitting Israel to return to their land to restore and build Jerusalem, to the time when the coming Messiah would be cut off (or crucified)—would be sixty nine of those sevens, or a total of four hundred and eighty three years. There should have been only seven more years for Israel to suffer for her past sins, before being restored to a position of divine favor. But because her Messiah would be "cut off," the angel went on to tell Daniel that the temple and the city would be destroyed (See Daniel 9:25-26). This was fulfilled as Daniel was told. After Jesus was crucified, the city of Jerusalem and the Temple were destroyed in 70 A.D.

I was once speaking with a Jewish woman and I asked her, "Since the God of Abraham, Isaac, and Jacob, informed the prophet Daniel though His angel Gabriel that Israel had a total of 490 more years to suffer for her past sins, and that this time period was to begin with a decree for Jews to return to their land and rebuild the city of Jerusalem (which occurred during the days of Cyrus, emperor of Persia), why is it that Israel hasn't yet been restored to divine favor under the rule of her Messiah? Why is it that Jews were forced from their land from the time of 70 A.D. when Jerusalem and the temple was destroyed by the Romans, and have suffered in exile among the nations for over nineteen hundred years since the time of discipline for past sins was to have been completed?" I then said, "Either the God of the Bible lied to you as Jews, or your people are suffering these many extended years for a worse sin committed by your forefathers. And that sin is that they delivered their own Messiah over to the Gentiles to be crucified. When they did so, they cried out, *"... His blood be on us and our children,(Matthew 27:25)."* I continued further to ask, "Could it be that this is the reason that you have suffered as a people for so long?" She rose up in her chair and exclaimed, "Then Jesus is the Christ!" I said, "Yes, Ma'am, He is!" I had the blessed privilege of baptizing her as a professing believer in the Lord Jesus Christ.

But wait! There are seven more years yet to be fulfilled of the total four hundred and ninety. What Daniel refers to as the time of "the end," or the final seven years remaining for Israel to suffer for her past national sins, would not begin until a prince that would come confirms a covenant with her for seven years. He would then break that covenant in the midst of the seven years, or after three-and- one half years. (See Daniel 9:26-27).

Theologians have traditionally called this a time of tribulation upon the nation Israel; the first 3 ½ years being a relative time of peace for Israel; and the second 3 ½ years as being a period of great tribulation compared to the first 3 ½ years. It is a time of suffering for Israel's past sins as a nation, and seems to be reserved for the very end of the Tribulation which is to come upon all the nations of the world. *It is additional suffering the nation Israel will endure on top of the suffering which is to come upon the entire world.*

The Total Time of the Tribulation

So it is clear that the prophets foretold of a time of Tribulation to come upon the world of nations, as well as a seven year time yet to be fulfilled of the four hundred and ninety years prophesied by Daniel for the nation of Israel. The question arises, "Are both times foretold by the prophets simultaneously and last only seven years, or does the seven year time prophesied by Daniel occur at the end of the Tribulation which is to come upon all the nations of the world?" And if the latter be true, how long will the total time period be?

The Lord Jesus Himself answers these questions in His Olivet Discourse. He refers to a "beginning of sorrows" to come upon the whole world. (See Matthew 24:3-8). He then describes a worldwide breakout of persecution upon anyone associated with the name of Christ, causing many to fall away from their confession of faith in order to save their lives from martyrdom. (See Matthew 24:9-13). Yet in spite of the effort by the nations to stamp out the name of Christ from the earth, "the gospel of the kingdom shall be preached in the entire world for a witness unto all nations." (See Matthew 24:14).

It is only after these occurrences that "the end" comes, according to Jesus in verse fourteen. The question arises, "What end? End of what?" Some have tried to say that Jesus is referring to only the last 3 ½ years, the first 3 ½ taking place before verse fifteen. This is because they regard the total time of the Tribulation as lasting only seven years. But the events described of martyrdom leading up to the time of "the end" do not match the description by the prophet Daniel of the first 3 ½ years. For it during that time that Israel should be protected from worldwide persecution, due to the seven year covenant with the Anti-Christ. So, it seems to be clear from a close examination of what Daniel said (see 9:26-27), that the prophet refers to the time of "the end" as being the total seven years left of the four hundred and ninety yet to be fulfilled. This would mean that the seven years prophesied by Daniel does not begin until the prior events Jesus describes leads up to it.

When the end, or the final seven years prophesied by Daniel begins, Jesus warns the nation in verse fifteen to not be deceived by the coming Anti-Christ. This is because, as has been stated, the first 3 ½ years should be a time of relative peace for Israel. But Christ warns them to be on the alert for the "abomination of desolation" to take place in the middle of the seven years (Daniel 9:27). It is at this time he is said to enter the temple in Jerusalem to proclaim himself to be god above all gods, puts an end to the temple sacrifices, and seeks to have all Jews annihilated.

After the final 3 ½ years of great suffering for the nation Israel, Jesus will return in the air for the whole world to see and will re-gather the nation of Israel from their places of hiding (See Matthew 24:16-31). So how long with the Tribulation last? It is at this point in the discourse, that our Lord reveals the total time period of the Tribulation. He states that, while no man knows the day or the hour, the generation living at the time when these things begin to happen, can expect to be alive at the time of the coming of the Son of Man, apart from their dying an unnatural death during the Tribulation.

Now learn a parable of the fig tree; When his branch is yet tender, and putteth forth leaves, ye know that summer is nigh. So likewise ye, when ye shall see all these things, know that it is near, even at the doors. Verily I say unto you, <u>this generation shall not pass, till all these things be fulfilled</u>. Matthew 24:32-34.

There is speculation as to how long a generation is, but this writer believes it to be a period of forty years, based upon God's judgment upon a generation of Jews in the past lasting forty years (Compare Hebrews 3:10). What this means then is this: that the Tribulation upon the world of nations, climaxing in the final time of the seven years for Israel to suffer under the Anti-Christ, <u>could last</u> up to forty years. The Lord does not say that it lasts only seven years, nor does he say when it begins (Matthew 24:36). But from what He does say, we know two things: that the Tribulation lasts <u>more than</u> seven years, and that it does not last for more than a generation, or a period of forty years. This extended time for the Tribulation allows for an interpretation of the chronology of events as described by John in the book of Revelation, to be taken in exactly the order revealed to him. This will be discussed in the next chapter.

So how long is the Tribulation? It is more than the seven year time period spoken of by the prophet Daniel upon the <u>nation of Israel for her past sins</u>. It is a time period to also include a time of suffering upon the <u>world of nations for their current sins</u> at the time the "day of the Lord" begins. And the generation of Jews living at the time when they see these things begin to be fulfilled, can fully expect to still be alive when the Son of Man returns.

The Mystery Revealed to the Apostle Paul

While the prophet Daniel told Israel exactly when the final seven years of the time of "the end" for them would begin, the prophets did not do so when foretelling the "day of the Lord" and God's coming wrath upon the total world of nations. Even our Lord, in describing the Tribulation, did not say when the "beginning of sorrows" would start. There is a reason for this. God waited to reveal to the Apostle Paul that it would be the sudden departure of the Church out of this world in the Rapture which would mark the beginning of the prophesied "day of the Lord."

It seems to be significant that the apostle Paul, to whom the mystery of the Church age was revealed, would also be the one to whom the mystery of the beginning the "day of the Lord" was also revealed. This is because the Rapture involves the Church. He describes the event of the Rapture to the Thessalonians (1 Thessalonians 4:13-18). He then informs them that the sudden departure of believers from the earth in the Rapture marks the beginning of the "Day of the Lord," at which time the world will be caught totally off-guard and will have no time to prepare for the terrible events that follow.

> *But of the times and seasons, brethren, ye have no need that I write unto you. For yourselves know perfectly that the day of the Lord so cometh as a thief in the night. For when they shall say, Peace and safety; then sudden destruction cometh upon them, as travail upon a woman with child; and they shall not escape. 1 Thessalonians 5:1-3.*

The fact that the apostle goes from the topic of the Rapture to immediately speak of the "Day of the Lord," has caused difficulties for those who have taught that the Rapture is immediately followed by the seven year Tribulation prophesied for Israel. If this were true, how would the world be caught by surprise, since the seven years are not to begin until Israel signs an agreement with the Anti-Christ? Such a compact would signal to even the most casual observer that the seven years had begun. On the other hand, there is no problem if one understands that the "day of the Lord," and the seven year "time of the end," as spoken of by the prophet Daniel, are speaking of two different time periods. Both involve a time of tribulation, but as has been said previously, one is for the whole world of nations for their sins at that time, and the other is for the nation Israel for her sins in the past..

The apostle goes on to say that believers in the Church Age should not be caught by surprise by the suddenness of the coming wrath to come upon the nations, because they are looking for the Rapture to occur at any moment of time to catch them out of this world when it begins.

But ye, brethren, are not in darkness, that that day should overtake you as a thief. Ye are all the children of light, and the children of the day: we are not of the night, nor of darkness. 1 Thessalonians 5:4-5.

Paul is taking these believers back to the symbolic meaning of the day. The original day of creation began with a time of night or darkness, followed by a time of daytime or daylight. In God's perspective, the day begins with darkness. This is why the Scripture says, "The evening and the morning were the first day," and so on. (See Genesis One). Paul is using an analogy to point out that the believers in the Church Age do not belong to the time of darkness and divine judgment to come upon the earth in the coming "day of the Lord," but they instead belong to the daylight that follows with the return of Christ to institute His coming kingdom upon the earth.

So in light of the fact that believers anticipate the Rapture of the Church at any time, and that it will occur at the same time when the day of the Lord's wrath begins to fall upon the nations, the apostle exhorts them to live as the children of the light before those who still belong to the darkness.

Therefore let us not sleep, as do others; but let us watch and be sober. For they that sleep sleep in the night; and they that be drunken are drunken in the night. But let us, who are of the day, be sober, putting on the breastplate of faith and love, and for a helmet, the hope of salvation. 1 Thessalonians 5:6-8.

"Hope of salvation?" What should cause the believers to whom Paul is writing to have a hope of salvation, or a hope of deliverance when speaking of the coming day of the Lord's wrath upon the nations? He gives the answer in the following verses:

For God hath not appointed us to wrath, but to obtain salvation by our Lord Jesus Christ, who died for us, that, whether we wake or sleep, we shall live together with him." 1 Thessalonians 5:9-10.

By the words "whether we wake or sleep," Paul is again referring to the Rapture, and God's purpose for it. And that purpose is to suddenly remove believers in the Church age from this world <u>before</u> the time of God's wrath is poured out upon the nations. *This is the mysterious disappearance.* This is what is meant by the term Pre-Tribulation. Fundamental scholars of the Bible believe the Rapture will occur before the Tribulation begins, based upon what the apostle Paul has to say concerning God's unique purpose for His Church.

The mystery of the Church and the mystery of the Rapture are in separately connected. God's program for the Church is distinct from His purpose for Israel. <u>To misunderstand the Rapture is to misunderstand the Church, and vice versa!</u> And to misunderstand the Rapture of the Church is to overlook God's revelation as to when the "day of the Lord" or Tribulation begins, as foretold by the prophets of old.

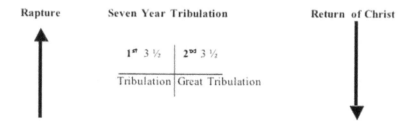

<u>Illustrative Chart of Traditional View</u>

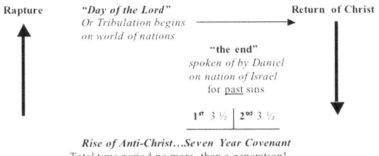

Rapture   *"Day of the Lord"*   **Return of Christ**
                     Or Tribulation begins
                     on world of nations

"the end"
spoken of by Daniel
on nation of Israel
for <u>past</u> sins

1st 3 ½ | 2nd 3 ½

Rise of Anti-Christ....Seven Year Covenant
Total time period no more, than a generation!
"this generation will not pass until..." Matthew 24:34

Illustrative Chart of Alternative View

Summary

So another reason the Pre-Tribulational Rapture is a fundamental doctrine to be guarded and cherished by the church today is because it is God's purpose to catch all believers away from this earth immediately, whether they are alive at the time or "dead in Christ," so as to be saved from the coming day of the Lord's wrath which will fall suddenly upon the nations of the world without prior warning or time for preparation.

The fact that the Rapture of the Church could occur at any moment, and the fact that the Lord's wrath will be poured out at the same time upon the world without fanfare, should be warning enough for unbelievers to not take chances with God in rejecting the Gospel of Jesus Christ. This is why Paul declares to the Corinthians that "now is the day of salvation; that "now is the accepted time." (See 1 Corinthians 6:1-2). Just as God shut the door of the ark, when the rain of divine judgment began to fall upon the world in the days of Noah, even so the door of opportunity to escape the future day of God's wrath will have passed with the Rapture of the Church. *Now is the time, if you have not done so, to call*

33

upon the name of the Lord Jesus Christ, asking Him to be your Savior. He is the one who came from heaven to die for your sins, and then rose again to give you life eternal. Pray and receive Him now before it is too late.

Having demonstrated that the total time of the Tribulation is more than the seven years prophesied by the prophet Daniel, we can now turn to the events as described in the last book of the Bible to see how this knowledge helps solve some disagreement between Pre-Tribulational scholars.

CHAPTER THREE

IT CORRESPONDS TO THE CHRONOLOGY OF FUTURE EVENTS AS REVEALED TO THE APOSTLE JOHN

Introduction

Scholars who hold to the Pre-Tribulation view <u>agree</u> that there is coming a day of the Lord's wrath upon the nations during the Tribulation, and they agree that Israel has yet to pay seven more years for her sins as foretold by the prophet Daniel. But they <u>do not agree</u> on the sequence of events immediately following the Rapture. Some hold that the seven year period begins immediately with the Rapture. Others believe that there has to be a gap or transition period of time between the Rapture and the final seven years, in order to allow time for the Anti-Christ to rise to power.

Neither do they all agree regarding the sequence of events as recorded in the book of Revelation. Some say that there is not enough time in seven years for all that is foretold to be fulfilled. Others note that the chronology of judgments do not fit within the two separate 3 ½ year periods described by the prophet Daniel. So they try to find some other way to explain how the chronology of events corresponds to those seven years.

Again, all of this becomes unnecessary when one realizes that the Tribulation lasts more than the seven years, as has already been established. Thus the chronology of the events recorded in the last book of the New Testament can be interpreted in exactly the order they are written. What follows is a brief overview of those events.

The Rapture of the Church

John was commanded by Christ to write the sequence of events in three major categories: "the things which thou hast seen, and the things which are, and the things which shall be hereafter." (See Revelation 1:19). The apostle complied by writing what he had seen in chapter one; a vision of the risen Christ in heaven giving him instructions to write the book.. In chapters two and three, John wrote of the Lord's separate message to seven churches in existence at that time, as His exhortation to all local churches during the Church age. These were "the things which are."

It is after this that John is told in the vision to "come up hither" in order to join Christ in heaven, and be shown things which "must be hereafter," (See Revelation 4:1). To this point of time in the vision, the Lord had allowed John to perceive of himself as still being on earth. So why is he commanded to join the Lord in heaven prior to revealing the sequence of events to follow? The answer is that the Lord does not want John to think of himself as still being on earth when the 1st seal of divine judgment is opened, beginning with chapter six. This is because John is an apostle of the Church, and the Church is not appointed unto wrath (as was pointed out in the previous chapter of this book).

John sees twenty-four elders seated around the throne of God, with robes of white and having crowns upon their heads. These represent the royal priesthood of the Church, even as twenty-four priests of the tribe of Levi continually served the Lord at the temple in Jerusalem. The elders not only give glory to God the Father as Creator in chapter four, but they celebrate the Lamb of God in chapter five. They celebrate Jesus Christ as that Lamb, because it is by His precious blood that people in the Church are saved out of every tongue, tribe, and nation, and will return with Him to reign as kings and priests upon the earth. (See Revelation 5:8-10).

The glorified Church, having been raptured in heaven, observe along with John as Jesus is given the seven sealed scroll to unleash the promised day of the Lord's wrath upon the earth. Those seals are then all opened, beginning with chapter six. But not one of them is opened until the Church has been caught up into heaven with the apostle John, so as to escape the time of divine wrath.

The Beginning of the Tribulation upon the World of Nations

Once the Church is taken up into heaven in the Rapture (chapers four and five), the Lord Jesus opens the first of the seven seal judgments. The rest of the seven seals are opened in sequence.

Seal One:	Revelation 6:1-2	Breakdown of world-wide political powers all at once
Seal Two:	Revelation 6:3-4	Wars worldwide all at once
Seal Three:	Revelation 6:5-6	Famines worldwide all at once

Seal Four: Revelation 6:7-8   Pestilences world-
                                                    wide all at once

One fourth of the world's population dies an unnatural death as a result of these first four seal judgments (6:8). The worldwide breakdown of political powers, the wars, the famines, and the pestilences described correspond to the "beginning of sorrows" Jesus mentioned in His Olivet Discourse. (Compare Matthew 24:6-8).

Seal Five: Revelation 6:9-11   First wave of world-
                                                   wide martyrdom
Seal Six: Revelation   Second wave
                    6:12-7:17   of worldwide
                                                   martyrdom

These two seal judgments correspond to the period of time leading up to the time of "the end" as described by Jesus (Matthew 24:9-14). It is interesting to note that there will be many saved as a result of the Rapture of the Church, but many of them will also be martyred.

A Special Warning: *While many will be saved after the Rapture, one must not think that he can deliberately reject the Gospel of Jesus Christ beforehand and still be given a "second chance" after the Rapture. The apostle Paul makes it clear that any who knew the truth beforehand and rejected it because they loved their sin, will all be damned, because they received not the love of the truth, that they might be saved. This will be discussed in the next chapter.*

In the sixth seal judgment, the Lord visits the earth with a worldwide earthquake, such as the world has never seen, and He will also visit the earth with worldwide destructive winds (after He first seals 144,000 Jewish men from harm to evangelize the earth, the Church no longer being present upon the earth). These severe judgments are designed by God to show the earth His great displeasure with their persecution of those who accept the Lord after the Rapture.

Due to the world's failure to heed these "beginning of sorrows," the Lord repeats what He did in times past to the nation Israel. He increases these judgments sevenfold, extending the seventh seal judgment to seven more trumpet judgments, (Revelation 8:1-6).

Trumpet One:	Revelation 8:7	1/3 of earth's vegetation burnt
Trumpet Two:	Revelation 8:8-9	1/3 of earth's sea and ocean water turned to blood
Trumpet Three:	Revelation 8:10-11 1/3	of earth's land water becomes poisonous
Trumpet Four:	Revelation 8;12-13 1/3	of earth's light darkened, both day and night

But as bad as this all has been, an angel is sent throughout heaven to warn the earth of the three Trumpet judgments yet to come. They are called the three "Woe" judgments. This is because for the first time God's judgment upon the earth involves creatures that come up from beneath the earth.

Trumpet Five:	Revelation 9:1-12	Scorpion-like locusts from the earth beneath

It is interesting that God who created locusts and scorpions, has the power to also create hybrid creatures in the earth beneath designed to judge mankind for their sin. Some would try to symbolize what is written, but John is not told any different as he is in other portions of the book (cf. Revelation 1:20). *Bible scholars should be very careful in reducing to symbols that which God might intend to be taken literally.*

If these creatures will literally appear on earth as described by John, it would make sense for any person reading of these future terrors to immediately accept Christ as personal Lord and Savior now, before it is too late. And would this not be God's intent in revealing these things? For God is "not willing that any should perish, but that all should come to repentance," (2 Peter 3:9).

Trumpet Six: Revelation 9:13-21   Snake-like horses
                                         from the earth
                                         beneath

The same can be said for these creatures as was noted in the comments regarding the scorpion-like locusts of the previous trumpet judgment. No wonder these are called "Woe" judgments.

Note that one third of mankind is killed as a result of the sixth trumpet judgment, Rev.9:18. Prior to this, one fourth of the world's population was killed as a result of the first four seal judgments (Rev.6:8). *This means that one half of mankind dies an unnatural death as a result of these judgments before the final seven years spoken of by Daniel is mentioned, beginning with chapter eleven.* This is truly a description of the "Day of the Lord" or God's coming Tribulation upon the world of nations for their sin, as foretold by the prophets of old in the Old Testament.

Interruption in the Vision, Revelation 10:1-11

Another mighty angel interrupts the progress of the vision to tell John that there will be seven more judgments yet to come during the sounding of the Seventh Trumpet. The news is both bitter and sweet. Bitter because of more yet to come, and sweet because after that time will be no more, and the time of these judgment will be over (10:5-7).

After this brief interruption, the progress of the sixth trumpet judgment continues into the eleventh chapter.

Continuation of the Sixth Trumpet Judgment Vision
The time of "the end," or seven final years <u>begins</u>!

The First 3 ½ Years

<u>The Events of Chapter Eleven Described</u>

This is the first time that the seven years prophesied by the prophet Daniel is mentioned by the angel to the apostle John.

And there was given me a reed like unto a rod: and the angel stood, saying, Rise, and measure the temple of God, and the altar, and them that worship therein. But the court which is without the temple leave out, and measure it not; for it is given unto the Gentiles: and the holy city shall they tread under foot forty and two months. Revelation 11:1-2.

The forty-two months mentioned refers to a 3 ½ time period. The same is repeated in terms of the Jewish calendar of 360 days, rather than 365 days.

And I will give power unto my two witnesses, and they shall prophesy a thousand two hundred and three-score days clothed in sackcloth, Revelation 11:3 (a score being twenty days, and threescore being sixty days,)

For 3 ½ years, God uses these two witnesses in the city of Jerusalem to pronounce plagues upon the nations of the world. They do so to express God's displeasure with the world for their acceptance of the Anti-Christ, and with Israel for a covenant that has been made with the Anti-Christ for her protection from the hostile Gentile nations. The Anti-Christ, referred to by Daniel as "the beast," is mentioned in this chapter, and the city of Jerusalem is regarded by God to be as "Sodom and Egypt" because of this covenant.

It is only after their ministry is completed during this time period that the Anti-Christ kills these two witnesses. The whole world celebrates as they observe their bodies lie in the streets of Jerusalem for 3 ½ days. But their mood changes from celebration to great fear, when they hear a voice from heaven saying "come up hither," and the two witnesses not only come back to life, but they ascend into heaven in the sight of the world. Perhaps a hundred years ago people might have tried to symbolize these events, but with today's modern technology one can understand how the world could look upon the bodies of the two witnesses lying in the streets of Jerusalem. Fear also comes to the world when they look upon the effects of an earthquake that occurs simultaneously in Jerusalem after the two witnesses have gone into heaven, killing seven thousand of its inhabitants.

A Problem in Interpretation for Those Holding the Traditional View

The fact that this is the first time in the chronological account that 3 ½ years are mentioned, presents a problem for those who believe that the total time period of the Tribulation lasts only seven years. Some have said that the events preceding chapter eleven refer to the first 3 ½ years, and the events of chapter eleven and afterwards refer to the last 3½ years. But that this must be the first and not the second 3 ½ years should be apparent for several reasons...

First, this is the first mention of 3 ½ years. It would seem plausible to think of them as being the first half of the seven years, and not the second. Second, the 3 ½ years mentioned here in chapter eleven still belong to the sixth trumpet judgment, whereas the 3 ½ years that follows in chapters twelve and thirteen belong to the seventh trumpet (see 11:15-19). This means that the 3 ½ years of chapter eleven, and the 3 ½ years of chapters twelve and thirteen are not the same, but two separate time periods. Third, while the city of Jerusalem and the outer court of the Temple are under the control of Gentiles, due to the covenant between Israel and the Anti-Christ at this time, the Jewish sacrifices in the inner court are still being allowed to continue during the 3 ½ years mentioned in chapter eleven. This corresponds with the first 3 ½ years, and not the last, as described by the prophet Daniel. For Daniel describes the last half as being a time period in which temple sacrifices are no long permitted. Fourth, when the seventh trumpet sounds, the Jews are no longer residing in Jerusalem, but have instead fled into the wilderness to a place where God hides them from the Anti-Christ, (cf. Revelation 12:6). They will do what Jesus told them to do, once the Anti-Christ commits the "abomination," (cf. Matthew 24:15-16).

So if the 3 ½ years mentioned in chapter eleven is the first half of the seven years prophesied by the prophet Daniel, and they are not mentioned chronologically in the book of Revelation until the sixth trumpet judgment, those who hold to the Traditional View of the Rapture being followed by only seven years of Tribulation have a hard time explaining where the previous seven seal judgments and five trumpet judgments fit into the sequence of events.

The Problem Resolved with the Alternative View

Is it not significant that the first 3½ years of the time period mentioned by the prophet Daniel are not mentioned until the time of the sixth Trumpet judgment? Is this not another source of biblical evidence that the total time for the Tribulation lasts more than seven years? The <u>alternative view</u> presented in this book resolves the problem of how to interpret the sequence of events, as recorded in the book of Revelation. There is no reason to squeeze all the events of the book into the seven years as described by Daniel. The Tribulation begins with judgment on the world nations, after the opening of the first seal judgment, and the final seven years prophesied by Daniel begins during the sixth trumpet judgment. The events can be interpreted to take place exactly in the order they are revealed to John and recorded by him.

The Second 31/2 Years

The sequence of events of the second 3½ years are given to the apostle John and recorded in chapters eleven through eighteen.

Chapter 11 The seventh trumpet, or third "Woe" judgment, is sounded. It is at this time that the tremendous persecution of Jews takes place. It can be assumed that the "abomination of desolation" is committed by the Anti-Christ at this time, because the Jews flee from Jerusalem for protection in the wilderness after the seventh trumpet has sounded.

Chapter 12 There is war in heaven between the devil and his angels, and the archangel Michael and God's angels, at which time the devil is defeated and cast down to be made visible to men on earth. (Compare Ezekiel 28:17). Knowing that he has but a short time, the devil seeks to destroy Jews who flee Jerusalem, but God protects them for 3 ½ years.

Chapter 13 It is at this time that all three persons of an unholy trinity appear before mankind on earth. The devil gives his throne and power to the Anti-Christ—who, as the second person of the unholy trinity appears to been resurrected from a mortal wound. And the False Prophet, as the third person, focuses the world's attention upon worship of the Anti-Christ. Note how the devil mimics the Holy Trinity (Father, Son Jesus Christ, and the Holy Spirit). The great worldwide persecution of Jews by the Anti-Christ for 3 ½ years is again emphasized.

Chapter 14 God warns the world, through the 144,000 Jewish evangelists He sealed during the sixth seal judgment, and through three angels who fly throughout the earth, not to worship the Anti-Christ or receive his mark. The world is told that the penalty for doing so is eternal burning in the lake of fire. Two sickle judgments follow upon the inhabitants of the great city of Babylon, where the image of the Anti-Christ will be set up.

Chapter 15 God again intensifies the seven Trumpet judgments into seven more bowl judgments. These are the judgments of which John was told would be the final seven (see chapter ten). The reason these judgments are brought to an end, is because the nation Israel and mankind in general would otherwise become extinct. This becomes obvious by the description given of these judgments. (cf. Matthew 24:21-31).

Chapter 16

1st Bowl: Grievous sores come upon all those in the world who worship the Anti-Christ and receive his mark. 16:1-2.

2nd Bowl: All sea and ocean waters become like the blood of a dead man. All sea creatures die. 16:3.

3rd Bowl: All land waters become blood. 16:4-7.

4th Bowl: All mankind is scorched by the sun. 16:8-9.

5ᵗʰ Bowl: Darkness comes upon the kingdom of the Anti-Christ. 16:10-11.

6ᵗʰ Bowl: The unholy trinity gathers the armies of the world to Israel, in order to fight in the battle of Armageddon against the anticipated return of Christ. 16:12-16.

Note: Some, who try to compress all of the judgments into seven years, have tried to associate the 200,000,000 horsemen of Revelation 9:16 with this account as part of the final battle of Armageddon. But this cannot be, in that the horsemen of Revelation 9:16 are part of the sixth trumpet judgment, while the armies of the kings of the east belong to the sixth bowl judgment. Furthermore, none of the bowl judgments begin until all seven trumpet judgments have been implemented.

7ᵗʰ Bowl: The greatest of all worldwide earthquake occurs, causing all the world's great cities to fall, and the mountains and islands to disappear. Hail, each stone weighing 100 pounds, falls upon mankind. The great city of Babylon upon whom the world's economy depends is divided into three parts. 16:17-21.

Chapter 17 The angel interrupts the progress of the vision again to inform John about another city called "Babylon" and how it will be destroyed. It is called a "mystery" because the city is not really the city of ancient Babylon, but another city which has perpetuated the idolatrous religion of ancient Babylon, the first Gentile world power (17:5).

This city was said to sit on seven hills and reign over the kings of the earth (compare 17:9 with 17:18). This city was guilty of shedding the blood of the saints. Five of its dictators had already fallen in violence (17:10).

That the apostle John would recognize this city as referring to the city of Rome is obvious. The city of Rome was also called "Babylon" in that day. The angel desired that John be comforted in knowing that this city, under whose reign he was suffering at the time he wrote this last book of the New Testament, would one day meet its end at the hands of the Anti-Christ and the ten kings in league with him (17:12-18).

Chapter 18 The angel resumes the progress of the seven bowl judgments by informing John how the future great city called "Babylon" will meet its final demise. Whereas the mystery city of chapter seventeen will be burned by the Anti-Christ and the ten kings united with him, it will be God Himself who will cause the city mentioned in chapters fourteen and sixteen to burn in one hour of one day, with fire from heaven (18:8). The world's merchants will mourn at the collapse of the world's economy due to the demise of this future city, where the image of the Anti-Christ has been erected (18:9-19).

Afterwards

The seven seal judgments, followed by the seven trumpet judgments, followed by the seven bowl judgments, set the stage for the Lord's personal return to fight against the armies of the unholy trinity that have been gathered together as of the sixth bowl judgment. The battle of Armageddon takes place in chapter nineteen. The Lord's reign upon this earth for one thousand years, followed by the Great White Throne Judgment, is the topic of chapter twenty, and the eternal state of the new heavens and new earth is the subject of the remaining chapters of the book.

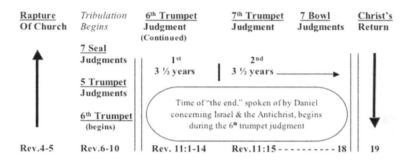

Illustrative Chart of Sequence of Entire Tribulation from Book of Revelation

Summary

When one understands that the Tribulation lasts more than seven years, it presents no problem to interpret the chronology of events as exactly as that revealed to the apostle John. This means that the Rapture of the Church occurs before the first seal of divine judgment is opened (chapters four and five); that the judgments begin upon the world of nations (chapters six through ten); and that these judgments are brought to a climax in the final seven years prophesied by the prophet Daniel, yet to be fulfilled upon the nation Israel (chapters eleven through eighteen). It is after this that the Lord returns to save Israel from becoming extinct as a people, and to establish His reign over the nations.

The fact that the Lord calls the apostle John to join Him in heaven in the vision before he is shown the "things which shall be hereafter," is another evidence for the Pre-Tribulation position. This doctrine is a fundamental because the Lord does not want the apostle to think of himself as being on the earth during the time of the vision when these divine judgments are poured out upon the world. Further evidence that the Pre-Tribulation Rapture is a fundamental doctrine is seen in a warning the apostle Paul gives the Thessalonian believers, pertaining to those who had come into their midst denying this doctrine.

CHAPTER FOUR

OF A WARNING GIVEN BY THE APOSTLE PAUL

Introduction

The apostle had already taught the doctrine of the Pre-Tribulation Rapture of the Church in his ministry to the Thessalonian believers, as has been seen in what he wrote in his first epistle to them. But he writes a second epistle to warn them against those who had come into the church claiming that the suffering they were enduring as a church for the cause of Christ was evidence that the Tribulation had already begun. Paul warns these believers to not be deceived by such claims (2 Thessalonians 2:1-2), to understand the necessity for the Rapture to occur before the Anti-Christ can have his say upon the earth (2:3-12), and to hold fast to the doctrine of the Pre-Tribulation Rapture as they had been previously taught (2:13-17).

Don't be Deceived by Those who would Deny the Pre-Tribulation Rapture of the Church

The saints at Thessalonica were indeed suffering persecution for their faith in the Lord Jesus Christ (see 2 Thessalonians 1:1-4). The apostle encourages them on the basis that God was allowing their present circumstances for a two-fold purpose: first, to prove their own worthiness to receive honor and prestige when Christ returns to this present earth to establish God's kingdom (1:5); and second, to demonstrate His own righteousness in judging all those who oppose the saints who believe in His name (1:6-12).

So Paul, on the positive side, wants these believers to be encouraged as to the purpose for God's allowing them to suffer for the cause of Christ. On the negative side, however, Paul does not want them to panic, because they somehow believe those who say that the suffering they are enduring is the beginning of the Tribulation, or "day of Christ," as had been foretold by Jesus and the prophets of old.

Now we beseech you, brethren, by the coming of our Lord Jesus Christ, and by our gathering together unto him, That ye be not soon shaken in mind, or be troubled, neither by spirit, nor by word, nor by letter as from us, as that the day of Christ is at hand. 2 Thessalonians 2:1-2

There are several things to note about this opening statement of chapter two. First, there are those who are saying that the "day of Christ" has already begun. The literal Greek rendering is the perfect tense of the verb "to come." Second, the term "day of Christ" is the same as the "day of the Lord" prophesied in the Old Testament, because Jesus Christ of Nazareth is that Lord being spoken of by the prophets. Whether or not the term is one of hope or one of panic depends upon to which portion of that day one belongs. If they be "children of the day" or of the day time, as Paul describes in his first epistle (1 Thessalonians 5:4-8), then the term is one of hope. This is because the believer looks forward to the coming of Christ and the salvation He brings at that time.

The apostle uses this term elsewhere in a positive sense when referring to believers in the Church (See 1 Corinthians 1:8, 5:5; 2 Corinthians 1:14; Philippians 1:6, 1:10, 1:16; and 1 Thessalonians 5:1-10). But here Paul is referring to the term "day of Christ" in a negative sense, in that some in the church are claiming that believers are going through the Tribulation along with the "children of darkness." In this case, the term "day of Christ" connotes a time of gloom, of darkness, and of divine wrath.

Third, when these believers remember how Jesus described the beginning of the Tribulation, one can understand why these believers are said to be on the verge of panic. Fourth, Paul appeals to these believers to not panic in remembrance of the coming of the Lord, at which time believers will be gathered together to meet the Lord in the air. For as Paul had previously written, the whole purpose for the coming of the Lord in the air for His Church, is to remove them from the earth when the "day of the Lord," or time of God's wrath, suddenly begins upon the earth.

So Paul begins his warning about those who would cause believers to panic, thinking that they were undergoing the Tribulation, by reminding them of his teaching concerning the Lord's gathering of His saints unto Him in the air before that time begins. He then reminds them of the necessity for the Church to be removed from the earth in the Rapture, before the world is made ready for the rise of the Anti-Christ.

The Necessity of the Rapture Prior to the Time of the Anti-Christ

The necessity for the Rapture to occur prior to the "day of Christ," or "day of the Lord, is three-fold: First, there has to be a worldwide falling away from Christianity, whereby the world will be receptive to the Anti-Christ when he is revealed (2:3-5); second, there has to be a removal of the present restraint against the kind of evil that will take place, once the Church is caught up to be with the Lord (2:6-12); and third, the promise God gives believers today in the giving of His Holy Spirit to those belong to Christ's Church (2:13-14).

The Necessity of the Pre-Tribulation Rapture in Light of the Coming Worldwide Apostacy

Paul moves to cite evidence to prove his point that the believers could not already be going through the Tribulation. His first evidence has to do with a tremendous departure of the influence of Christianity in the world that will take place once the Rapture of the Church occurs.

Let no man deceive you by any means: for that day shall not come, except there come a falling away first, and that man of sin be revealed, the son of perdition Who opposeth and exalteth himself above all that is called God, or that is worshipped; so that he as God sitteth in the temple of God, shewing himself that he is God. Remember ye not, that when I was yet with you, I told you these things? 2 Thessalonians 2:3-5

According to the apostle Paul, the believers of Thessalonica could not already be going through the Tribulation, because there would have to be a "falling away first." The Greek

word is *apostacia,* from which our English word "apostacy"
is derived. It literally means "to depart from," and refers in
this context to a departure from the influence of Christianity
in the world today due to the Rapture of the Church.

Does not this word summarize what conditions will
be like in the world once the Tribulation begins? Did not
Jesus describe those conditions to His disciples in the Olivet
Discourse? Did He not say that it would be a time when
many false Christ's would arise (Matthew 24:4-5)? That it
would be a time of worldwide persecution and martyrdom
of many who profess the name of Christ (Matthew 24:9-12)?
And did He not say that these things would have to take
place before the time of the Anti-Christ and his persecution
of Israel as spoken of by Daniel (Matthew 24:14-16)?

What Paul is saying to the church at Thessalonica is
this: "Yes, it is true that you are suffering for the name of
Christ. And yes, it is true that some of your loved ones have
died for their faith. But no! It is not true, as some are telling
you, that these are signs that the Tribulation has already
begun, because what you are experiencing is in no way to be
compared to what Jesus said would be conditions worldwide
in the beginning stages of the Tribulation."

The Necessity of the Pre-Tribulation Rapture
In Light of the Present Restraint Against Evil

How can the "Man of Sin" have his way upon the world
with the Church still present on earth to oppose him? It is
this second argument to which the apostle then directs the
attention of the Thessalonian believers.

And now ye know what witholdeth that he might be
revealed in his time. For the mystery of iniquity doth
already work: only he who now letteth will let, until
he be taken out of the way. And then shall that Wicked

be revealed, whom the Lord shall consume with the spirit of his mouth, and shall destroy with the brightness of his coming: Even him, whose coming is after the working of Satan with all power and signs and lying wonders, And with all deceivableness of unrighteousness in them that perish; because they received not the love of the truth, that they might be saved. And for this cause God shall send them strong delusion, that they should believe a lie: That they all might be damned who believed not the truth, but had pleasure in unrighteousness. 2 Thessalonians 2:6-12.

The word translated "letteth" in verse seven is the same in the Greek as the word "witholdeth" in the previous verse. It means "to restrain." Paul says that the "mystery" involving iniquity is that while it is present on earth at the time he writes, yet it will not be allowed to progress to worldwide dominance under the Anti-Christ, until "he who lets," or restrains, is removed.

Who is that restrainer, and what is meant by his removal? Well, what has Paul been talking about? Has it not been the "gathering unto Him" of His Church out of this world in the Rapture before the beginning of the Tribulation (2:1-2)? And is it not the Church age, Spirit-indwelt believer, who is the restrainer? Did not Jesus tell His disciples that when the Holy Spirit had come to indwell them, that their lives would become a source of conviction to the world of sin, of righteousness, and of a coming divine judgment for its sin (John 16:7-11)?

Yet when these Spirit indwelt, and Spirit controlled believers from all over the world, are instantaneously caught up in the Rapture and removed from this earth, that restraint will no longer be present. The world will become much more receptive to the wicked and deceptive ways of Satan and the Anti-Christ at that time.

The Necessity of the Pre-Tribulation Rapture
In Light of God's Promise to His Spirit-indwelt Church

How fearful it would be for believers in the Church to be told they will go through the Tribulation, or any portion of it? Who would not panic, if they thought the apostacy and "beginning of sorrows" Jesus foretold had begun? Even worse, should they be present on the earth when the Anti-Christ begins his rise to world power. For Paul says that the Satanic signs and wonders being performed at that time will be very deceptive (2:9-12).

But how comforting it is to know that true believers of the truth will not be deceived at that time, because they won't be here! They will have already been removed from the earth in the Rapture.

> *But we are bound to give thanks always to God for you, brethren beloved of the Lord, because God hath from the beginning chosen you to salvation through sanctification of the Spirit and belief of the truth: whereunto he called you by our gospel, to the obtaining of the glory of our Lord Jesus Christ. 2 Thessalonians 2:13-14.*

Paul begins verse thirteen with the conjunction, "but." This is to set up a sharp contrast between those left behind in the Rapture and are deceived, because they had previously rejected the truth of the Gospel, and those to whom he is writing who have believed and are saved. He says that they are "beloved of the Lord." He says that God has chosen them to be saved, or delivered from the terrible times that would come upon the earth when the Anti-Christ has his way for a season upon this earth. He says that the proof of this is that they have been sanctified or "set apart" unto God in receiving the indwelling Spirit of God, and that this occurred when they believed in the truth of the Gospel (in contrast to those "left behind" in the Rapture who rejected the truth). These believers will have obtained the "glory" of the Rapture by which they are removed from the earth and escape the terrible events to follow.

Summary

So here then is a fourth reason for asserting that the Pre-Tribulation Rapture of the Church of Jesus Christ is a fundamental truth of the Bible pertaining to prophecy. For it is has been shown that the apostle Paul defends this doctrine, and challenges those who would say otherwise. In fact, he warns them to not be deceived by anyone regarding this, even should the apostle himself write a future epistle denying this fact. He then adds these words at the close of chapter two:

Therefore, brethren, stand fast, and hold the traditions which ye have been taught, whether by word, or by our epistle. 2 Thessalonians 2:15.

If the apostle Paul goes to such great length to defend the doctrine of the Pre-Tribulation Rapture of the Church, warning against any who would deny it, and then tells them to "hold fast" to what they have previously been taught regarding this, would it not seem reasonable to conclude that this truth is a fundamental doctrine of biblical prophecy to be guarded and protected?

There is yet a fifth reason to present on why this is a fundamental doctrine of biblical prophecy.

CHAPTER FIVE

IT IS THE BASIS FOR THE BELIEVER'S COMFORT TODAY

Introduction

Paul gives three reasons to the believers at Thessalonica for their being comforted by the doctrine of the Rapture of the Church.

The first is that they do not have to sorrow "as others who have no hope." For the fact is that, due to the Rapture, death will not separate them from their loved ones who have died in the Lord. In the Rapture, the "dead in Christ will rise first."

> *But I would not have you to be ignorant, brethren, concerning them which are asleep, that ye sorrow not, even as others which have no hope. For if we believe that Jesus died and rose again, even so them also which sleep in Jesus will God bring with him. For this we say unto you by the word of the Lord, that we which are alive and remain unto the coming*

of the Lord shall not prevent (or precede) them which are asleep. For the Lord himself shall descend from heaven with a shout, with the voice of the archangel, and with the trump of God: and the dead in Christ shall rise first. 1 Thessalonians 4:13-16.

Furthermore, they might still be alive when this occurs. For they will be caught up to join them in the air without having to go through the experience of death themselves. That this could take place at any moment is observed in the fact that the apostle includes himself as possibly being one of those still alive when the Rapture takes place.

Then we which are alive and remain shall be caught up together with them in the clouds, to meet the Lord in the air: and so shall we ever be with the Lord. 1 Thessalonians 4:17.

Paul tells them to comfort one another with these words when experiencing the loss of their loved ones in death.

Wherefore comfort one another with these words. 1 Thessalonians 4:18.

A second reason for comfort is that the Rapture will take place suddenly, the purpose being to remove believers who are still alive from the earth in order for them to avoid the sudden wrath that will catch the world totally by surprise. The apostle speaks of the sudden beginning of the Tribulation immediately following his comforting words concerning the Rapture of the Church.

Paul reiterates that the Rapture is a basis for comfort in chapter five. This time it is with the emphasis that God will remove believers in the Rapture prior to the sudden beginning of the "day of the Lord." This is because believers in the Church are not appointed to experience the wrath of God when it falls upon the world of nations.

> *For God hath not appointed us to wrath, but to obtain salvation by our Lord Jesus Christ, Who died for us, that, whether we wake or sleep, we should live together with him. Wherefore comfort yourselves together, and edify one another, even as also ye do. 1 Thessalonians 5:9-11.*

By the words "whether we wake or sleep," it is obvious that Paul is making reference back to the topic of the Rapture he had mentioned previously in chapter four. Just as the Rapture is a doctrine of comfort concerning separation from loved ones who have died in the Lord, it is also a source of comfort in knowing that its suddenness will save believers from the day of God's wrath to come upon the nations.

Then in his second epistle to the Thessalonian believers, Paul gives a third reason for the doctrine of the Pre-Tribulation Rapture being the basis of the believer's comfort today. God will remove His Church from the earth, not only to avoid experiencing the terrible times he terms as the "falling away" which precede the coming of the Anti-Christ, but also to avoid being deceived by the tremendous signs and wonders that will be used by Satan to cause the world to believe the lie of the Anti-Christ.

> *Now our Lord Jesus Christ himself, and God, even our Father, which hath loved us, and hath given us everlasting consolation and good hope through grace, comfort your hearts, and stablish you in every good word and work. 2 Thessalonians 2:16-17.*

What a contrast to Paul's opening words in chapter two! There he deals with the fact that some in their midst were saying that the Tribulation had already begun, and he speaks of the emotional panic they were experiencing in believing this false teaching. He urges them to "not be soon shaken in mind, or be troubled, neither by spirit, nor by word, nor by letter as from us, as that the day of Christ is at hand" or had already begun.

Having defended the fact that the Church will be gathered up into heaven and removed from the earth prior to the events of the Tribulation, now the apostle can encourage them on the basis of "everlasting consolation and good hope through grace." The doctrine of the Pre-Tribulation Rapture of the church, he says, is the basis for comforting their hearts. It also enables them to be stabilized in their emotions to concentrate on serving the Lord, rather than on their personal survival, for he goes on to say, "... and stablish you in every good word and work.

In other words, Paul concludes each section of his teachings on the Rapture with a word of comfort, (1 Thessalonians 4:18, 5:11, and 2 Thessalonians 2:17). That word of comfort is based upon his emphasis that the Rapture of the Church precedes the Tribulation which is to come upon the world.

CONCLUSION

There can be two approaches to setting forth an argument to prove one's position. One is the negative approach in which one challenges all the assertions made by those of the opposing viewpoints. The other is more positive, and that is to simply set forth one's viewpoint in such a convincing way that it is not necessary to go into detail regarding other viewpoints. This latter approach is the author's preference.

For this reason, alternative viewpoints which deny the Pre-Tribulation eschatological position have not been discussed. This writer's preference has been rather to explain the prophetic Scriptures in such a way as to build a strong defense for holding on to the Pre-Tribulation position as one of the fundamental doctrines of the Christian faith.

This discussion does not disclose the sources of some disagreements between Pre-Tribulation scholars over the sequence of events immediately following the Rapture of the Church. Rather, it presents an *alternative view* that helps to resolve some of the disagreement, <u>but is still within the Pre-Tribulation viewpoint of eschatology.</u>

In these days it would be easy for believers to panic, especially when we observe the wicked direction in which the world seems to be heading. But the doctrine of the Pre-Tribulation Rapture of the Church will help us to keep looking up for the imminent return of the Lord for His Church, as well as to keep focused upon serving the Lord with the comfort of knowing that—as bad as things may be—the Church will be removed by the Lord before the day of His wrath begins.

If the concept of the Rapture causes fear to rise in the heart of the reader, this fear can be removed by calling upon the name of the Lord Jesus Christ now to be your Lord and Savior while the door of salvation remains open for you. The title "Lord" means that you accept the claims by Jesus of Nazareth to be the divine Son of God. This means He is the only man born on earth that you worship as your God.

The title "Jesus" means "Savior," and was the name given to him by God at his birth (Matthew 1:21). The Lord Jesus had to be born in the world as a man in order to go to the cross and die for the sins of the world. The fact that He is both God and man is the reason the payment of His shed blood on your account is valuable enough in the sight of God to forgive all yours sins, as well as all the sins of all sinners who believe on His name for their salvation.

The term "Christ" corresponds to the Hebrew title "Messiah," meaning God's Anointed One. The Lord Jesus did not stay in the grave. He rose from the dead to give everlasting life to all who will put their trust in Him, and He will return to this earth to reign forever as "King of kings, and Lord of lords."

With this information in mind, humble yourself to do the following as commanded in Scripture, and God promises in His Word that you will be saved from the wrath to come.

That if thou shalt confess with thy mouth the Lord Jesus, and shalt believe in thine heart that God hath raised him from the dead, thou shalt be saved. For with the heart man believeth unto righteousness; and with the mouth confession is made unto salvation... For whosoever shall call upon the name of the Lord shall be saved. Romans 10:9-10, 13.

If you obey God's command in Scripture after having read this book, it would be a special blessing for this writer to hear of your decision and for further lessons to be given you to help you grow in your Christian life. Simply write: *Dr. Daniel Carfrey, Appalachian Bible College, P.O. Box A.B.C., Bradley WV, 25818.*

Jesus closed out the book of Revelation by saying to John that He would soon come. We would say with John, believing these words to be true, "Amen. Even so, come Lord Jesus." (Revelation 20:21).

CPSIA information can be obtained
at www.ICGtesting.com
Printed in the USA
BVHW032204310821
615768BV00005B/121

9 781606 476833